STEP INTO THE LIGHT

Adrian Stepp

Light Publishers LLC
Annapolis, Maryland

Step Into The Light

Copyright © 2008, 2017 by Adrian Stepp
First edition 2008. Revised edition 2017

All rights reserved. No part of this publication may be reproduced, distributed or transmitted in any form or by any means, including photocopying, recording, or other electronic or mechanical methods, without the prior written permission of the publisher, except in the case of brief quotations embodied in critical reviews and certain other noncommercial uses permitted by copyright law. For permission requests, write to the publisher, addressed "Attention: Permissions Coordinator," at the address below

Light Publishers LLC

1900 Annapolis Exchange Parkway Suite 300

Annapolis, Maryland 21401

www.lightpublisher.com

Ordering Information:
Quantity sales. Special discounts are available on quantity purchases by corporations, associations, and others. For details, contact the "Special Sales Department" at the address above.

ISBN: 978-0-9995272-0-7 (pbk)
ISBN: 978-0-9995272-1-4 (ebk)

Printed in the United States of America

CONTENTS

Dedication i
Acknowledgments ii
Introduction iv
Chapter One: Blueprint 6
Chapter Two: Foundation 22
Chapter Three: Preparation 32
Chapter Four: Tools 42
Chapter Five: Diving In 50
Chapter Six: Acceptance 58
Step Into the Light 63
About the Author 65

DEDICATION

This book is dedicated to my family:

My mother who has gone home to be with the Lord, whose unconditional love, guidance, and mentorship have been the wind beneath my wings. My daughters and grandchildren whose unwavering support have caused me to go on further.

ACKNOWLEDGEMENTS

First, I want to give honor and glory to GOD Almighty Who is worthy of all praises. I acknowledge that GOD alone gets all the Glory for this divinely inspired work. I also would like to thank the many people that have poured into my life throughout the years. The support, encouragement, the time shared with me, your thoughtfulness, your kindness, your warmth, and your love given to me in order for me to be where I am now. My Pastor Bishop Don Meares at Evangel Cathedral, my church family Evangel Cathedral I love you all so much. I truly appreciate the love you have given me. My brothers and sisters in the Prison Ministry, Men's Prayer ministry, Security ministry, you all have taught me so much I love you. And of course, Circle of Champions, Minister Bob Yates what an awesome work GOD is doing with your ministry. Thank you so much, and all the others that I didn't name but certainly have not forgotten. Thank you so much.

INTRODUCTION

The world has moved fully into the information age, and with that has come an unprecedented expansion of accessibility. With the touch of a few keys on a computer, one can access nearly any information they want on the Internet. This movement however, which has been growing since the turn of the century, has reached a point at which spiritual laws and principles are being violated continually, without any regard to consequences. Society is seemingly numb to the dangers, or worse yet, passive to the mindset. This is a mindset that is destined, unfortunately, to steal, kill, and destroy the very fabric, the very essence, of mankind. This movement is, ultimately, an enemy of man.

This book, borne and inspired out of love for my incarcerated brothers and sisters, whom I have had the privilege to minister to, will explore this movement and its consequences. Through my interaction with inmates, I came to learn of the serious problem that is bringing destruction to the very fabric of our society. Men and women are truly being attacked on all levels. But this battle is a spiritual one. It cannot be fought physically. Therefore, we must look at another alternative in order to triumph over this movement. "Step Into The Light" is the key to unlocking and breaking the cycle of that movement.

CHAPTER ONE

Blueprint

The mind of God is awesome. There is no promise man can make that can compare to the unbreakable, unconditional, unfailing love of God. Man's word can break. It can let you down. God's word will never let you down. Only God's report is worth believing in and holding onto, because it will never fail you.

By faith we know that the world was framed by the power of God's word. That same word informs us that we have been created in God's very own image. What this means is that you and I are already blessed. We are blessed simply because of who we are: God's very own. We are the true children of God. Throughout the scriptures, this point is made clear, beginning with Genesis.

> *"And the Lord God formed man of the dust of the ground, and breathed into his nostrils the breath of life; and man became a living soul."* (Genesis 2:7kjv)

Everything that man needed was given to him in the Garden of Eden. But man disobeyed, which left him cutoff from God. Things became very hard for man at that point. There was no light in his life. Disconnected from God, life became a struggle to make ends meet.

But God, in His love for the world, had a plan of redemption for mankind. God's plan was to give us His son, Jesus Christ, who would redeem mankind from his sins and reconnect him to the spirit and presence of God. This good news is what the New Testament writers exclaim in their letters and testaments. Perhaps John captures the joy of this good news the best, when he says: "whosoever believes in Him will have everlasting life and will not perish. (John 3:15) Hallelujah! Glory to God! Thanks be to God for His Son Jesus Christ.

John goes on to remind us that "those who believe in and receive Jesus Christ will be given the power to become the sons of God." (John 1:12kjv) Jesus himself confirms this, when he says, "Except a man be born again, he cannot see the kingdom of God." (John 3:3kjv) This is vital. We must be born again from the Holy Spirit in order to experience, to get to know the kingdom of God. Once we are born again, God assures us that He will sprinkle clean water upon us, and we shall be clean from all our filthiness, and from all our idols. We will be given a new heart and a new spirit. We know this from the words of Ezekiel.

> *I will sprinkle clean water on you and make you clean instead of unclean. Then I will cleanse you from all your idols. I will give you a new heart and put a new spirit in you. I will remove your stubborn hearts and give you obedient hearts. I will put my spirit in you. I will enable you to live by my laws, and you will obey my rules.* (Ezekiel 36: 25-27)

Only in Him and by Him are we able to live such a life. Without Him there is no life or light at all. The Apostle Paul makes this point clear in his letter to the Philippians.

> *"I can do all things through Christ who strengthens me."* (Philippians 4: 13 kjv).

John also writes about the supremacy of God's word and the light that brings to those who believe.

> *In the beginning was the word, and the word was with God, and the word was God. The same was in the beginning with God. In Him was life; and the life was the light of men. That was the true light, which lighteth every man that cometh into the world. And the word was made flesh, and dwelt among us, (and we beheld his glory, the glory as of the only begotten of the father,) full of grace and truth. "The law was given by Moses, but grace and truth came by Jesus Christ. (John 1: 1-4, 9,14, 17 kjv)*

If we believe in Jesus Christ, the scriptures assure us that we will have life everlasting. This is truly good news. God also says, "whosoever drinks of the water that I shall give him shall never thirst; but the water that he shall give him shall be in him a well of water springing up into everlasting life." (John 4: 14)

Hallelujah! If you have not yet done so, now is the time to come into agreement with God's truth concerning your life. Say to yourself what God says about you. These words from God are the truth. There is no need to entertain any other notion as to our true identity. We are God's.

God tells us that His thoughts about each of us are more than all the grains of sand on the earth. Think about that. If you take a bucket of sand and try to count each grain, you would never be able to. But God's thoughts toward you and I are more than all those grains of sand. Amazing!

What are His thoughts? Jeremiah tells us the answer to this question:

> *"I know the thoughts that I think towards you, says the Lord, thoughts of peace, and not of evil, to give you an expected end."* (Jeremiah 29: 11)

These words are refreshing because now you know that God is not out to harm or hurt you. God only wants to love and bless you.

The big question is, what does this word of God look like in our lives? Well, in order to travel, you must know the direction in which you are going. It is the same with our spiritual journey. To arrive at our destination, it is vital to have light. Light gives us the ability to see the course before us. It is very difficult to move in darkness without light. Something bad is bound to happen. Without light, we lack direction. And without direction, we risk becoming stagnant in our spiritual development and maturation. Of course, the light I am referring to is Jesus Christ. He is the light of the world. In Him is life and without him there is no life (light). God has a plan and a purpose for each one of us. In Him we live, move and have our being. We are all part of the body of Christ. Just as Jesus Christ is the light of the world, so are we able to show unbelievers the way to the true living God.

This is because, by reflecting the light of Jesus Christ in our lives, we succeed in shining the light of God's love and truth into the world. Christ is our model. We copy his steps, his ways, his actions, his behavior. We become the very picture that we see in him. We behold Him and all of His Glory. God has imprinted His ways and His plans on our hearts. We actually have been given everything that we need to live for God. It was given to us before the foundation of the world. It is written in our hearts, imprinted by God Almighty Himself.

It is important to understand that the love He has for us is greater than anything we can imagine. Everyone who is born in this world has DNA. They also have a spiritual DNA. That spiritual identity is lying inside each of us, waiting to be revealed, waiting to be tapped into. The imprint that is within us goes far beyond anything you can imagine in the natural. As a matter of fact, the natural man cannot understand or receive this type of information. God has placed answers inside each of us that no one can fully comprehend. The wisdom and power that God has put into our hearts is truly indescribable. God only wants what is best for us. We must trust Him and believe Him. We must keep His word in our heart, so that we will not sin against Him.

Hold on to the word inside of you. Hold on to it tight. Never let it go.

This seed of God's light was planted in Jesus before the beginning of time. It withstood all the tumult of creation and the fall of mankind. At an appointed time the seed began to push up through the earth. No one knew what the seed would become except the planter (God). The planter faithfully watched over the seed. He fed it, He watered it, and He gave it increase. Then the seed began to establish the foundation in which it was intended. He grew and grew, bigger and taller, stronger and wiser. He became a man. He grasped hold of the plan and purpose for which he was sent. He performed all sorts of miracles and wonders. Signs followed everywhere he went. People from all over marveled at His presence. He was able to open and close doors that no other was able to do. And He is like that now, able to open and close doors that no one else is able to. The power of the seed is awesome. We must embrace Him if we want to be victorious in life.

Every part of our bodies can be used to connect to this light of God. Our eyes are extremely important, as they enable us to see what is needed to move. Ears are vital also, because they enable us to hear what we need to hear in order to move. Our mouth is crucial also, because we are able to speak that which we hear with our ears and see with our eyes. The mouth is especially interesting because of the power that was given to it by the planter (God). It can bring about life or death. Kind, loving words bring joy and life into the world. Harsh, rude, or untrue words bring about pain and death. Hopefully you will choose life. God intended for you to use your mouth for life.

The point is, we must be sensitive in our hearing in order to speak the things that God has in store for us, and to activate the promises and inheritance that is offered to us. Our eyes must be fixed on God's purpose, so that our ears can hear what has been said about that promise, and our mouths can release what we've seen or heard. This is truly

Blueprint

an awesome responsibility. And when each one of us is in harmony with God, miraculous things begin to take place. All of a sudden the limits are gone. There are no boundaries to what could happen or take place in the name of God.

Everyone is given this opportunity to accept the seed (Word) that the planter (God) has planted. All should embrace this seed, for it is essential for mankind to live. Without the seed, mankind will perish. Of course, we would be in existence, but not in the manner that would be profitable or beneficial or pleasing to God.

Of course, not everyone will embrace the seed. But why must we be ignorant or stubborn when signs are all around us beckoning us to come forward to accept His son? What a catastrophe it would be to realize too late that the seed is alive and real, that it is here now for the accepting. How awful, how frightening that would be to believe the lie instead of the truth. In the seed is life. All that is good and wholesome and pure is in the seed. There is nothing else outside of the seed except frustration, confusion, doubt, torment, unbelief, worrying and death. Who wants that?

Unfolding the blueprint (seed) in our lives is fairly easy. It takes a decision to be obedient. It takes making a strategy for how to follow the course that is given to you by God. You'll find out that as you unfold the seed, new doors and opportunities will become available. A whole new life will unfold before you. It is challenging, refreshing, rewarding, and exciting to follow the map that is given to you. And as you pass through the deserts and valleys and mountains of your life, you will witness something interesting taking place within you. You will find a peace that passes all understanding. You will become more confident and trusting in the map that God gives to you. Your spiritual journey can be fun! Imagine having your very own tour guide with you all the way of your life! He knows all the good spots and knows where all the jewels and nuggets are. The guide is so good he even lets you know about the traps and pitfalls so that you can avoid them. God is good!

Understanding the tools that you have to use is a must in order to use them properly. When you do use these tools properly, your heart will be in right alignment with the seed. Part of using your tools well is to be prompt in obeying when hearing. To understand your tools is to allow your actions to reflect your words. As you embrace these tools that God has planted within you, I want to encourage you to hold steadfast in your heart to the vision of God's spoken word. Stay with it. Don't let it go. Continue on always, speaking when prompted by the word to do so. Don't say anything that is contrary to God's word. This is a must for you to do. Stay in remembrance of Christ, as the apostle Paul urged us to. Be patient with yourself. Reward yourself for the steps that you have made thus far. It's getting brighter and brighter each day. Every day you are coming closer to the prize.

Blueprint

Just keep at it and use your tools properly. Always rely upon the word to direct, guide, lead, and keep you. Rest in the word, knowing that outside of the word is death, lies, frustration, confusion, doubt and unbelief. Hold on to the word in your heart. Protect the word within you, lest it risk being taken away from you by the tendencies of this world. Do as the scriptures say and put on the whole armor of Christ. This will protect you from any and everything that is contrary to the word. Never take your armor off. Your armor is your covering. Store the word safely in your heart. Guard it night and day. Watch what you allow to enter into your heart. Do not give access to things that are contrary to the word. Shelter yourself from the undesirable elements. Watch the company that you keep. Sometimes you have to cut people off, stop relationships or end bad habits in order to protect the word. It is only for your good. Remember that God, in His word, knows what is best. You can trust the Lord with your whole heart. When you cover and shelter the seed properly, it will always produce.

Blueprint

Sometimes thirtyfold, sometimes sixtyfold, and sometimes a hundredfold.

Always put God first. He'll work wonders for you. But to do this you must know the word of God. If not, you risk planting the wrong seed, which will yield the wrong harvest. For example, you cannot plant tomato seeds and expect to get corn. You reap what you sow. The incorruptible seed of God's word is the seed that you want. Even though you will be challenged or tempted by different seeds, you must choose the incorruptible seed every time over the other seeds. Watch out for counterfeits. Trust the word.

The elements will come against you. But if you are clothed properly, they can't harm or hurt you. For example, imagine that you are in your car and it is raining heavily outside. But the rain is not raining on you, because you are on the inside of the car covered and protected. The corruptible seed will be like you are in a convertible car with the top down and it is pouring down rain. You will not be covered or protected at all.

Don't build or start anything without the word of God first. It is neither smart nor wise. It is foolish to build without the word because it won't last. It is an accident waiting to happen. It is like building a house without a blueprint or foundation. The house will go up, but it won't stay up because it has no foundation or structure to support it when the elements come against it. Be smart. Check with the word first. Whatever you do, do it according to the word, which will protect you against any storm. It is like building your house on rock, as Jesus told us to do, rather than shifting sand.

CHAPTER TWO

Foundation

The word of God is what gives structure to our lives. This structure is like a solid rock that does not crumble or break under pressure. It will hold up or support you during troubling or turbulent times. No other foundation is stable or solid like the word of God. It is imperative, therefore, that you have a solid foundation. If you embrace the word, your foundation is sure to stand. It is sure to support you in every area of your life, from now to eternity.

The word gives the stability and the hope we need to keep on in spite of adverse circumstances or situations we may face. In order to maintain this foundation in your life, you must take time to ponder and meditate on the word. By so doing, you will grow deep roots, which will not be easily uprooted. You will develop a lasting and stable foundation to support every aspect of your life, and unlock the passion, energy and enthusiasm that God has planted within you. This foundation can be found only in the word of God as revealed through Christ Jesus. Look unto Him. Keep your eyes fixed, set, anchored, rooted, grounded on Him at all times. This is a must. Then He, the carpenter, will show you how to build. He will build you up. He will make you, shape you, mold you in whatever area you need to be shaped or molded. But you must allow Him to have His way in your life. There is power, real power, in the word. You can call on Him at any time. He is always there for you. He loves you more than you can ever realize. He wants to bless you.

Study the word daily. Let the word take first place in your life. Let it have priority over all that concerns you in every area of your life. Make a decision to be committed to the word at all times no matter what the cost. For this is our duty to be obedient, just like Jesus was obedient even unto death. Look unto Jesus and ask Him to come in and sup with you. Read your bible regularly (preferably daily). This will give you a chance to get to know Him in more depth, and to build a closer relationship to the mind and heart of God. What will follow is an intimate relationship with Him.

This is the same recipe for building any solid relationship. In order to get to know your spouse intimately, you must spend time with him or her. It is the same for our relationship with Jesus Christ. By accepting and receiving the terms of His word, we allow for a solid foundation to be established in our lives.

The scriptures tell us that if we believe and don't doubt, we can have whatsoever we ask for in prayer. This is a true saying. My question to you is, what are you asking? Are you asking what the word says? Or, are you asking things that don't have the word as their foundation? You must be willing to embrace the word. When you do finally receive the word, you will develop a peace that passes all understanding. A void will be filled in your life. A void that you may not even know you had. This is a void that can only be filled by Jesus Christ. Without receiving Christ Jesus, you will never be truly fulfilled. You will never have real peace or lasting joy.

There was nothing made or created that was not by Him. He is the very essence of our being. He is the creator of all creation. He is the God above all gods. There is no other beside Him. He is alpha and omega the beginning and the end. He is the author and finisher of our faith. It is vital to be in Him. Without God there is no life or truth. There is no truth outside of Him. There is no force or power or counsel that is mightier than God.

He rules supreme. He is sovereign. He is omnipotent. He is omnipresent. He is omniscient. He is the true and living God. He is the great I Am, Lord Jehovah. God

Foundation

Almighty. He is King of Kings and Lord of Lords. To understand this, is the beginning of wisdom. The word of God is powerful. All that is ever needed can be found in the word. Anything and everything that you could ever imagine or need answers to is encoded in the word. You must have faith that the word of God is true. Without faith, it is impossible to please God.

The Bible will be your guide to unlocking and accessing the indestructible word of God. It is an extremely valuable tool to help you with your faith development. Your faith, when built upon the right foundation, will literally allow you to move any mountain out of your way. Above all, always remember that the word is very potent. Unlimited power lies in the word.

Hold fast to your confession of faith always. This foundation gives you strength, support and stability. The potential for God's seed to grow and develop in your life is limited only by the limits you place on your faith.

Your mouth is a great tool. But you must learn how to use it properly. It can take you to incredible, unimaginable heights. It can also betray you. Be careful to never sow seeds that are contrary to the word of God.

Pondering is a must, to ensure that your faith is not limited. You should always ponder over your feelings as to where God's seed is leading you. Ponder and meditate. By doing so, you will gain revelations from God. You will be able to see how to take hold of the direction God is leading you and to decipher the clues God is offering you. As Proverbs says, "commit your works unto the Lord, and your thoughts shall be established. (Proverbs 16: 3kjv). In other words, take time to meditate on the word day and night. In all your ways, acknowledge Him, and He shall direct your paths. This is a true saying. Do not enter in with doubt or hesitancy Enter in with faith that when you live by God's word, it will succeed in your life. God says if you are willing and obedient, you shall eat the good of the land. In this truth, you can always trust.

Foundation

It is also important to recognize that faith without works is dead. You must do the works with your faith. Be relentless in your pursuit. Don't let up. Be on the lookout for cracks in your armor. An unwillingness to forgive is a crack in your armor. Bitterness, or being easily offended are cracks in your armor. Anger and resentment are also cracks that can develop in your armor. If you don't take care of cracks like these, bigger problems can come about as a result. Once your foundation becomes faulty, you have no strength. At that point you have gone overboard, abandoned the word and become lost in the affairs of your own will, not God's. This leaves you extremely vulnerable for a major catastrophe to happen. Of course, the good news is that you don't have to stay on that route. You can confess your sins and ask for forgiveness.

So, guard your heart. Be a watchman. Do not give anything access to your heart, if it is contrary to the word. Hold on tightly to the word, always remembering and watching for the word to produce fruit in your life, because it is alive all the time. The word works every time. It helps you to make intelligent decisions. It is a guide to assist you in making choices. Jesus is righteous. Jesus is holy. Jesus is honorable and magnificent. Jesus is glorious, wonderful, almighty, powerful, and victorious. He is the Truth, the Way, and the Life. Always build your foundation on the word from the very first. As long as the word is held or used in its rightful position, you never have to worry or be concerned. By doing and keeping the word, you put yourself on the pathway that will keep peace in your life. Being faithful and obedient will bring about a joy that is unspeakable, because of the intimate relationship you have with God. In His presence is fullness of joy. Only by His word are we made righteous. Understanding this helps you align to the righteousness in which He has made you. There is only one truth. Accept this understanding of your true self to be exactly who God says you are. Reject what the world may tell you you are. Both cannot be true. You are who God says you are, which is His beloved child. This truth is truly wonderful to embrace. Hallelujah!!!

Foundation

31 | Step Into the Light

Chapter Three

Preparation

It is wise to prepare. In order to build or make anything, it is necessary to prepare. The same is true for the building of our spiritual lives. The word tells us, warns us, and instructs us throughout the bible to prepare. Preparation ensures that you have the necessary tools, plans, or ingredients to bring about the outcome you have in mind. It is very wise, for example, not to go to war without first seeing if you are able to overcome your enemy with what you have. If you want to bring about the truth of God's word, we need to first prepare ourselves in that word.

Understanding the importance of preparation

will enable your project to run a lot more smoothly. The outcome of a project that is built upon a foundation of solid preparation will always be positive. Believers are commanded to prepare in the word. We need to prepare to make sure that we are setting things properly, from God's perspective. When believers prepare themselves in the word as instructed, there is no limit to what they can accomplish or do. No limit, because God is working with you and through you. Of course, the best time to prepare is now. If you put the word first in your life, you will always be prepared to live out God's word in your words and actions.

Part of preparation is study. The word tells us to study. "Study to show yourself approved unto God, a workman that needed not to be ashamed, rightly dividing the word of truth." (2Timothy 2:15kjv). The amplified version of that scripture goes further:

Preparation

> *Study and be eager and do your utmost to present yourself to God approved (tested by trial), a workman who has no cause to be ashamed, correctly analyzing and accurately dividing (rightly handling and skillfully teaching) the Word of Truth."* (2 Timothy 2:15 amp).

This presents an even clearer picture of the importance of preparation. By preparing properly, you will be equipped to handle any and all situations or circumstances that you might face. You will be able to put into action the steps you need to take. You can draw from your knowledge of the word to recall pertinent truths that shed light on your situation. Once in the light, you will decipher a detailed plan of action to take. Gathering and studying requires a certain measure of discipline on your part. But the rewards are worth the effort. When you are prepared to act according to your knowledge of the word when any situation comes your way, you ensure that you stay rooted on the only true and lasting foundation.

Never forget to absorb the word day and night. Meditate on it. Chew on it. Your mind must be continually renewed all the time. With discipline and commitment, you create an expectancy to achieve or accomplish that for which you are preparing. This requires disciplining yourself to study and prepare, especially when you don't feel like it. You already do a lot of things now that you don't feel like doing.

Learn how to rechannel that energy. Begin to focus on those things that are good, wholesome, positive, and constructive. Your mind will support and help you when you stay in line with the word. It is amazing how things begin to unfold for you when you are aligned with the word. Once you embrace this kind of discipline, your mind will prepare you to set new standards, new heights for yourself.

Being ready is good for you, because when an opportunity becomes available, you are already ready for it. You don't have to waste time getting ready. You are already ready. This kind of self-discipline will set you up for great opportunities in the future. You are ahead when you are ready. The word tells us to be ready all the time. Learning to be obedient to the word is the key. Commit to be committed and you will be victorious. Stay in the word all the time. Coming out of the word should not be an option. Stay locked in it. It is a marvelous light that reminds you of the victory you have already won. Don't just date the word. Marry the word. There is nothing that can be compared to this marriage. It is the ultimate high. It is the ecstasy of ecstasies.

When you prepare your heart properly for the word, you need to be sure to also guard it and protect it. Be very careful what you allow to come into your heart. You do not want thorns or thistles to grow in your heart. Renew your mind constantly according to the word. Ask God to show you who you are in the word. When you are truly in love with your spouse, no one from the outside can make you cheat. There is no temptation, because of the depth and sincerity of your love. It is the same with the word. If you have ever been touched by God, you can't help but to be in love with

Preparation

Him. His love is irresistible. Yes, feelings might come up against you. Circumstances or situations might prop up to hinder you in your relationship with and preparation in the word. But if you stay true to the word. even though ungodly thoughts will pop up, they will not consume you.

Make sure that your motives are pure and clean according to the word. Correct your steps, according to the word, being obedient to do as commanded and expected. Make sure that you are diligent in your work by taking correct steps of action. This is good because when you do things with correct actions and a pure heart, things pretty much will pan out for you.

There is nothing wrong with not knowing how to do or start something. We do not know it all. But the word tells us to seek counsel. Of course, you don't want counsel from just anybody or anyone. The word tells us not to seek ungodly counsel. This kind of counsel is not good for you. Make sure that your steps

Preparation

are good, that they are planted on the solid ground of God's word. Embrace and abide in the word all the time. This cannot be overemphasized. This is vital for a believer or anyone. Herein lies the hidden treasure, the earthen vessel. Keep it pure and clean. Keep your thoughts, your hands, yourheart, your mind, your body, and your spirit focused on the word.

We've all had to overcome difficulties. But in looking at where you are in life today, what do you see? Do you see old patterns from the past continue to recur in your life? Are bad behaviors, bad tempers, dishonesty, lying, stealing, cheating or abusing part of your life? There is a way to stop those behaviors from recycling through your life. You don't have to stay on a road to nowhere. The word allows you to turn around. By following the word, you will be put on a course you always wanted to be on, but never knew how. You will have a good roadmap to avoid the pitfalls and trap. The word is the light that will allow you to see clearly. Now you will have a vision, a purpose. Your relationships will become a lot better and more meaningful. Life will be much more enjoyable with family and friends. And, you will begin to love yourself. If you haven't been in touch with yourself for a long time, it will feel good to come back home again. It will feel wonderful to find peace within yourself.

We can get into comfort zones at times, and become hesitant about moving beyond those comfort zones. The unknown or unfamiliar becomes an excuse for staying within the confines of our comfort zone. God has a lot that He wants to do in us and through us. But we must let Him have his way in our lives. We must be willing to trust Him in the new, unknown, unfamiliar experiences we face. Taking steps using the word is the best choice you can ever make. When you do it that way, your steps will be directed. They will be ordered. But always be sure to take time to listen to what God is saying, and then move accordingly. This is why a continual focus on the word is so important, because God's timing is always right on time!

Patience and perseverance are critical. Don't try to do everything all at once. Be content with taking baby steps. Eventually you will take bigger steps. What matters is that there is no truth outside of the word. By concentrating on the word, you are always seeking, looking, asking, knocking to get the guidance you need to take the next steps in your life. When you focus on the word, you are in His presence, inquiring in His temple. How awesome it is to be in His presence. Relaxing in His presence, there is not a care or concern. It is truly described as Joy Unspeakable.

Getting married is an excellent way to stay focused and be committed to your marriage. When you are completely in love with your mate, you become fixed, settled if you will. There is nothing outside of that marriage. No desire, no interest. Likewise, you must come to a place where you have no desire or interest to do anything outside of the word. You must

Preparation

become fixed on the word. It is like the breath in your body, which you can't live without. There is literally nothing impossible when you are focused and the word is settled in you. I strongly recommend that you marry the word. That is the best way to stay focused at all times. Divorce is not an option.

Because you are not abandoning the word, when storms arise, they will not unsettle you, because you are settled in the word. There is nothing more powerful than love. Embracing love and being committed to love will keep you safe. When you do, you will be free. You will have peace. Your joy will be full. Life will take on a whole new meaning. When your relationship with God is truly intimate, you will be able to really trust and live in the word. Now is the time.

Chapter Four

Tools

You will need many tools to step into the light. You will also need to know when to implement these different kinds of tools. Wisdom is the principal ingredient to successfully implementing the word in your life. Of course, the bible is the best tool you can have. It is accurate in every facet of your life. It provides a road map for your spirit. Your hands and your mouth are also incredibly important, powerful tools. With the bible as their foundation, they can be tremendously effective tools in your efforts to make the love of God real in your life.

But to do so, you must make up your mind to

use the word the right way. Be sober and diligent in using your tools properly. With the foundation laid, you can use your tools to erect the structure of God's plan and purpose for your life. Applying the word rightly will set you up in places or positions that only God could have done.

But now you must decide what you are going to build. What are you going to put together? What are you going to set up? You must choose to build according to what the designer (God) intended. The bible is the best place to discover your purpose. It is your store, your shopping center, if you will, for your soul. Everything that you could ever need or imagine is in the store. In this store there is no rust, no moths, mold or mildew. There is no corruption. It is solid and airtight. God's word can't be broken into, stolen or taken away. There isn't a better place for you to discover yourself, than the bible.

It's time to use your tools to discover your true purpose in life. It's time to build your house in God's word. Are you still living in a tent? Have unwanted guests been occupying your house? Have they not treated your house well? Did they misuse and abuse your home? Is your house now in shambles? Such unwanted guests are never authorized to use our homes. But when we are asleep, not paying attention to the word, they can creep in. So, even if your house is broken down, decaying, and rotting, the good news is you have tools to rebuild!

It's time to take your rightful position as the owner of the house. Chase the unwanted guests from your house, then take your tools and rebuild, renovate your house. Restore it to its original design and purpose. You have all the materials that are needed to rebuild in the manner that it was supposed to be. Being the carpenter that you are, it will be fun and rewarding to see your house a home to God's word again.

A craftsman is an expert in his trade. So it is with you, when you have learned and understood the working of the word. You are a craftsman when living in the word has become a way of life. A surgeon undergoes many years of schooling to become a skillful surgeon. Likewise, being in the word for many years allows you to become a spiritual craftsman. Start everything that you do with the word of God. By faith, believe that you have received what you asked of him. If you are not sure what to do, stand firm in waiting. Don't rush to make something happen on your own, it will most likely come back to haunt you. Remember what the word says, "trust in the Lord with all your heart; and lean not unto thine own understanding. In all thy ways acknowledge Him, and he shall direct thy paths." (Proverb 3: 5,6kjv).

As you ponder the word of God, it will become clear to you what tools you need for each task. Even though the answers may not always be clear immediately, be patient and have perseverance. Seek earnestly the things that you need, based on the word of God, and they will be made known to you. Ponder and meditate. When using the right tool, the desired results will follow. They may even be better than expected!

What tools do you need, for example, to read the bible? You need good lighting. You should have a concordance, dictionary and bible. If you use glasses, you will need those too. All of these ingredients, these tools, will help ensure that you are fully prepared to read the bible and get the most from it. There is so much to be gained if we draw from the word. If we allow the word to be our source, our store, our warehouse, there is no end to the ways that God can take root in our lives.

You can always trust the word. The word is freeing. It is refreshing. It is an incredibly wonderful source of life that God has given to us. Always keep your tools clean. Polish your tools regularly after every use. Keep your tools sharp, so when it is time to start cutting, your tools will not be dull. Stay in the word in season and out of season. As long as you stay prepared, you are ready for anything that comes along. The word of God assures us that we can have boldness and confidence when we use the tools that He has given.

Isn't God wonderful? What joy it is to have a relationship with the Lord. It is truly an unspeakable joy. God makes this clear from the first lines of Genesis.

> *In the beginning God created the heaven and the earth. And the earth was without form, and void; and darkness was upon the face of the deep. And the Spirit of God moved upon the face of the waters. And God said, Let there be light; and there was light. And God saw the light, that it was good; and God divided the light from the darkness.* (Genesis 1: 1-4kjv)

It is clear from this scripture that God always wanted light separated from darkness. He does not want you to walk in darkness. The light is where we need to be. If there are dark areas in your life and you can't seem to find your way, turn to the word. Let there be light in your life, and it shall be. God has called us to walk uprightly before Him and in doing so He has promised to not withhold any good thing from us. But we must walk uprightly. He commanded us to be Holy as He is Holy. We know that He is coming back again, so we rid ourselves of those things that are not like Him. Because we are the sons of God, we know that when He shall appear, we shall be like Him; for we shall see Him as He is. And every man that has this hope within himself, is purified, even as He is pure.

Jesus has said that He is the light of the world. Jesus says that those who follow Him shall not walk in darkness, but shall have the light of life. We are the sons of God. We are truly the light of the world and the salt of the earth. You need to understand that your relationship with the Father through His son can be fully awesome. We should not trade it or sell it for anything. I love Him so much. He is my everything. How about you? Is He your everything? There is none like Him. He is ever so wonderful, faithful, righteous and holy. Remember what John says:

> *"The thief cometh not, but for to steal, and to kill, and to destroy; I am coming that they might have life, and that they might have it more abundantly."* (John 10:10kjv)

Therefore, gird up the loins of your mind, be sober, and hope for the grace that is to be brought unto you at the revelation of Jesus Christ. Be his obedient child, not fashioning yourself according to the former lusts in your ignorance. God is faithful. He is an excellent provider, an excellent landlord, an excellent firm foundation, a solid rock upon which to build your life. God is Light, and in Him there is no darkness at all. Stay in Him, rest in Him, walk in Him, live in Him, move in Him, abide in Him, trust in Him, lean on Him, rely on Him and adhere to Him. Walk in the light, as He is in the light, so that we will have fellowship with one another. The blood of Jesus Christ cleanses us from all sin. We are God's workmanship, created in Christ Jesus to do good works.

CHAPTER FIVE

Diving In

So, are you tired of being frustrated in life? Are you tired of being confused? Are you tired of being tormented, and not understanding the fight that you are in? Trying to fight a spiritual battle physically, will never get you victory. You must learn to fight the good fight of faith, by effectively using the word of God. In order to do that, you must spend time in God's word. Get to know your rights as a believer. Get to know what was left in the will for you. Get to know your inheritance, your benefits, your rights. Learn how to use the keys that have been given to you. Understand the authority and power that was given you. Learn how to use your authority as a believer. Start to enjoy the benefits of the kingdom. Are you wondering how to keep the enemy under your feet? Do you want to know how to heal the sick? Would you like to be able to move mountains out of your way? Then, it's time for you to step into the light.

In all your ways acknowledge Him, and He shall direct your paths. Trust in the Lord with all your heart; and lean not on your own understanding. We are alive only through Jesus Christ our Lord. In Him we live, and move, and have our being. Do you want to be made whole? Then rise and walk. Speak no guile, for the Lord is against them that do evil. But he that lacks an understanding of God's character is blind. Because God loves us unconditionally, we ought also to love one another. There is no fear in love. In fact, perfect love casts out fear. A very wise man once told me that love is the key. As simple as this sounds, it is 100% true. Love is the key that opens and closes doors that no one can shut or open.

God is love. Walk in love, abide in love, rest in love, trust in love, adhere to love, rely on love, set in love, be fixed in love. Let love be your motivator. Let love be your educator. Let love be your peacemaker. Let love be your compass. Let love be your counselor. Let love be your pilot. Let love be your director. But seek ye first the kingdom of God, and his righteousness, and all these things shall be added unto you. This is true. The Lord delights in you. Let us hold fast to the profession of our faith without wavering, for He is faithful. This is a promise in which you can trust! Hallelujah!!! Glory to God.

Strive to live in peace with everybody. Strive to share love. Strive to be God's ambassador on this earth. Faith without works is dead. For as the body without the spirit is dead, so too it is that faith without works is dead. Submit yourself to God. Resist the devil. If you are humble before God, He will exalt you. Allow the word of Christ to dwell in you richly, that you may obtain true wisdom for your life. If we only knew the love that God Has for us and took the time to fully understand it, we would be extremely happy to be obedient. We would have no problem doing as He has commanded us to do. All of His thoughts towards us are always good. They are never evil. He has the best plan and purpose laid out for our lives already. What we must do is trust that plan and purpose that He has for us. For example, take a parent who loves their child deeply and tries earnestly to teach that child what is best for him. By trusting the parent, the child then can come to see that their guidance was accurate. They will come to be grateful for such loving parents. God himself is that same parent who has laid out a blueprint on how to live in this world.

God loves us and wants to guide us. The paths God has for us are beautiful. God only wants the best for you. God is a faithful, righteous, wonderful counselor, and can truly be trusted. There is no other truth outside of Him. So therefore, you can be fully persuaded, fully confident, fully bold in the things that God has spoken to you. He will do exactly what He

Diving In

says He will do. What an honor it is to have a real relationship with the one that created everything. Amazing!

I love God and I know that God loves me. He talks with me, walks with me and calls me the apple of His eye. Oh, what a wonderful relationship. I don't date Him anymore. I have married Him. There is none other that can please or satisfy me like Him. I have no desire for any other. He is truly my everything. God is the complete package: nothing missing, nothing broken. Step into the light. Try Him for yourself. You have tried some of everything else. But if you have never really given Him a try, now's the time. How can you say something bad or doubt Him, if you have never given Him a chance? Ask Him today, to come into your life. Tell Him you want to know Him for yourself. Tell him that you want to get to know Him personally. Assure God that you will allow Him to order your steps. Tell God that you will allow Him full access to every area of your life. Tell God that

Diving In

you will rely and depend on Him. Say this prayer out loud:

Jesus, I ask you to come into my life now. I am a sinner. I realize that I need you. I am nothing without you. God, you said in your word, that if I confess with my mouth that Jesus is Lord, and believe in my heart that you raised Him from the dead, I will be saved. So, by the integrity of your word, I confess now with my mouth that Jesus is Lord. I believe in my heart that you have raised Him from the dead, and now I am saved. Thank you, God, for saving me. Thank you, Jesus, for being my Lord and my Savior. Thank you so much.

By saying this prayer, you have entered the kingdom of God. You have been born again and you will have full access to the kingdom. I recommend that you find a local church and get involved. If you haven't been baptized, do so. If you don't have a church home, you can email me or write me. Praise God, heaven is rejoicing today over you. A new soul has

Diving In

come into the kingdom. Hallelujah!!! Glory to God.

Diving In

Chapter Six

Acceptance

God is the fountain of life. In His light, we shall we see light. God has called man to walk uprightly before Him. We are not able to do this by ourselves, but we are able to do this through Christ who strengthens us. Blessed are those that know this joyful sound, for you shall walk in the light of His countenance.

Here is a little test: think about what's bothering you right now. Finished? Ok, now think about praising God. Here's the point: you can't praise God and think about negative things at the same time. God inhabits the praises of His people. When God shows up the enemies are scattered. They can't stay in His presence. What a mighty God we serve. It

Acceptance

is vital for us to accept His way of doing things, if we want to live the good life that He has predestined for us before the foundation of the world. Think for a moment if we had to choose to believe God or man: which one would you choose? Your answer should be a no brainer. But how often it is that we choose the ways of man over God. But why would we do this? Why would we choose man over God, who is worthy of all honor, glory and praise? This thinking is warped. If I asked you now to cheer for your favorite team, you'd scream loud without hesitation. But then if I asked you to give a shout for the Lord, I would need a crowbar to pry your mouth open. This shouldn't be. No one should be praised or glorified more than the Father God. There is nothing wrong with respecting and giving honor to others. But it should never be above that of the praise we give to God. No one has the right to that highest place or position but God Almighty Himself. He alone is worthy of that position. He is the God above all gods.

Acceptance

I encourage you to stay in His presence at all times. Be bold, confident in the Lord God Almighty. Know that God always hears your prayers. The scripture assures us of these things.

> *And this is the confidence (the assurance, the privilege of boldness) which we have in Him; (we are sure) that if we ask anything (make any request) according to His will (in agreement with His own plan), He listens to and hears us. And if since) we (positively) know that He listens to us in whatever we ask, we also know (with settled and absolute knowledge) that we have (granted us as our present possessions) the requests made of Him.* (1 John 5: 14,15 amp).

Hallelujah!! Glory to God, the giver of such good news. God is Light, and in Him is no darkness at all. Step Into the light. Whosoever shall confess that Jesus is the son of God, God will live in you, and you in God. Those people will know that God has given us eternal life. This is an absolute truth. It is not based on whether you believe it to be true. It is a fixed law. It was established before the foundation of the world. Consider, for example, the law of gravity. If you jump off a building, you will fall to the ground every time. It is a law. So, it is with the word. If you have the Son, you have life (Christ). If you do not have the Son (Christ), you don't have life. This is the truth put very simply. All you have to do is say "yes" to Him. All you must do is say "yes" to His will, "yes" to His way. What are you waiting for? Step into the light today!

What joy it is to be connected to the true living God. It gives a peace that surpasses all understanding. How wonderful it is to be exactly where God would have you to be, doing according to His perfect plan and will for your life. This is the place He has called all of us to be. This is where all your provisions, happiness, joy and peace are to be found. It is like being back in the Garden of Eden, before the fall. What an awesome God we serve. I am in complete awe of Him. I can only understand a little of what the angels were saying about Him to one another, but it is no wonder that they shouted out to Him, "Holy, Holy, Holy." I literally can't imagine the awesomeness of God, because He

Acceptance

supersedes any thought that I may have of Him. There is none better than God. Step into The Light!!!

Step Into The Light

This organization seeks to helping people live a more fruitful and productive life, by showing them biblical principles that will greatly enrich their lives greatly. We want people to be able to experience joy, peace, and happiness in their everyday lives, based on sound doctrine and principles of scripture that have been tried and proven over the centuries.

"But ye are a chosen generation, a royal priesthood, an holy nation, a peculiar people; that ye should show forth the praises of Him who hath called you out of darkness into His marvelous light.' (1 Peter 2:9 KJV)

"All scripture is given by inspiration of God, and is profitable for doctrine, for reproof, for correction, for instruction in righteousness: that the man of God may be perfect, thoroughly furnished unto all good works." (2 Timothy 3:16,17 KJV)

"God is not a man, that He should lie; neither the son of man, that He should repent: hath

He said, and shall He not do it? Or hath He spoken, and shall He not make it good?" (Numbers 23:19 KJV)

About the Author

Adrian Stepp resides with his wife in Grasonville, Maryland. He is the father of four daughters and the grandfather of ten grandchildren. He is a member of Evangel Cathedral in Upper Marlboro, Md., where he is a faithful servant in the Security ministry. He is the founder and CEO of "Step into The Light Ministry."

www.ingramcontent.com/pod-product-compliance
Lightning Source LLC
Chambersburg PA
CBHW021136300426
44113CB00006B/450